RN FRIGATES

K525

Lt Cdr Ben Warlow RN

Author's Notes

My Grandson, Alex, aged six, said to me "Grandpa, come and sit down, and tell me all about frigates." As always, Grandad has to obey, and this is the result.

At the outbreak of the Second World War, the Royal Navy was desperately short of escort vessels. A stop- gap vessel, the Flower Class corvette, was introduced. Small and handy, these vessels were manoeuvrable and could be built in quantity by many of the smaller shipyards in the United Kingdom. As the war developed, it became clear that a larger, faster vessel was required. A design was prepared, and was known as the 'twin screw corvette'. At the suggestion of Vice Admiral Percy Nelles, Canada's Chief of Naval Staff, the name was changed to 'Frigate', evocative of the small ships of Nelson's era. Then, they were 28 to 36 gun vessels that were the size smaller than 'ships of the line'. Their task was vague and rather all embracing, and with cruisers they were the eyes of the Fleet. In the Twentieth Century the new frigates role was, initially, that of convoy escort, but rapidly became "all embracing" too.

These new frigates were far more habitable than the Flowers, had more speed and twice the endurance, some 7,000 miles at 12 knots. The RN versions were named after rivers, and the RCN units were named after towns and cities. These vessels were a resounding success, and welded vessels to the same design were built in America (Colony Class). The subsequent class was designed to be of the same size, but of prefabricated construction, allowing more rapid building. The average River took 15-18 months to complete, whilst the Lochs took 10-11 months. This class, the Lochs, also carried the new ahead throwing anti-submarine mortar, Squid. A variation of the Lochs was built for anti-aircraft duties, with two twin 4-inch guns and with the lighter Hedgehog anti-submarine mortar instead of Squid. Some of this class became survey ships, and others, depot ships. At the same time, in America, a destroyer escort was produced, faster and relying on hedgehog and depth charges for anti-submarine work (Captain class). These were called frigates in the Royal Navy.

Post war the fleet was re-organised, and the sloops and Hunt Class destroyers were included in the collective term 'frigate', together with the Castle class corvettes. These corvettes had been built in parallel with the River and Loch class frigates. Slightly larger than the Flower class corvettes, to accommodate the Squid anti-submarine mortar, they were smaller than the frigates and were designed to utilise the shipyard capacity that could not build the larger frigates.

First published in the United Kingdom in 2004 by Maritime Books, Lodge Hill, Liskeard, Cornwall, PL14 4EL

HMS ANNAN 25.9.1944

ANNAN was built by Hall Russell, Aberdeen, and completed in March 1944. She, like RIBBLE served with the Royal Canadian Navy from 1944-1945, sinking U-1006 in October 1944 off the Faeroes and rescuing 44 of her crew. After her return to the Royal Navy in June 1945, she was transferred to the Danish Navy, She was renamed NIELS EBBESEN on 27 November 1945 and was employed as a boys' training ship. She was broken up at Odense, Denmark in 1953. Note the single four inch guns fore and aft, the radar mounted at the rear of the bridge and heavy depth charge armament aft. ANNAN was one of the class fitted with a cowl at the top of her funnel.

As submarines were being developed with higher underwater speeds, a counter was required. The Lochs and earlier ex-sloops and ex-corvettes were recognised as being too slow for modern actions. Some fleet destroyers were taken in hand for conversion to the anti-submarine role. A limited version, Type 16, carried Squid and a twin 4-inch gun, whilst a fuller conversion (Type 15), carried the same armament, but with a modified bridge structure incorporating a massive operations room. Some of the later conversions to Type 15 carried the longer range Limbo anti-submarine mortars. A Type 18 was projected as an improved limited destroyer conversion with two Limbo mortars and anti-submarine torpedo tubes using the old N class destroyers. This type was to be developed after trials of the Type 15s, but was not carried further. Another proposal was for a Type 62 Aircraft Direction destroyer conversion using the old M class destroyers and other emergency war design destroyers on the lines of the Type 15, but, again, this was not pursued.

These vessels were stop-gap measures, and a new-build programme was started in the 1950s. A small anti-submarine frigate for rapid production (Type 14) was introduced, together with a larger, more heavily armed version (Type 12). At the same time an AA frigate (Type 41) and an Aircraft Direction frigate (Type 61) were built followed by a general purpose frigate (Type 81). The last introduced improved living conditions (including dining halls) and also carried a helicopter. The Type 12 were followed by a slightly improved Rothesay class, which in turn was followed by the Leander class, which carried a helicopter, and formed the backbone of the Fleet for many years.

Another development was the Type 21, relying on gas turbine engines (which had been tried in the Type 14 frigate EXMOUTH), and incorporating ideas by Vosper Thornycroft. These smart looking ships were popular with their crews. The next frigates were the Type 22, relying on missiles for offence and defence, and again powered by gas turbines. These vessels were the size of pre-war cruisers, and later versions were fitted with a 4.5inch gun as a result of lessons learnt in the Falklands War.

They in turn were followed by the Type 23 frigate, whose fine lines indicate their stealth characteristics, so necessary to hunt the modern, quiet submarines and not be detected by enemy sensors. The last Type 23 was completed in 2002, and no new frigates have been ordered, though there has been much speculation as to the type of vessel to follow, with suggestions of a catamaran hull. Whatever new vessel finally is built, it is to be sure that the lack of frigates will be bewailed by modern admirals as much as it was by Nelson.

And so, Alex, does that answer your question? Perhaps some photographs would help…..

Ben Warlow
Burnham on Crouch
2004

Note: All photographs are author's collection except where indicated. 'WSPL' indicates World Ship Photo Library, 'MPL' indicates Maritime Photo Library and 'PRNM" indicates Portsmouth Royal Naval Museum.

HMS AVON

The AVON was completed in September 1943 by Messrs. Charles Hill and Sons, Bristol, having been laid down 8 months before. This photograph shows the depth charge throwers and rails that covered the quarterdeck, but these ships also carried the hedgehog ahead throwing mortar for anti-submarine work. She served in Western Approaches and in January 1944 deployed to the Eastern Fleet, operating in the Indian Ocean and Bay of Bengal. In January 1945 she joined the British Pacific Fleet and escorted the Fleet train. She was placed in reserve at Devonport in May 1947. She became the Portuguese NUNO TRISTAO in May 1949 and was broken up in January 1970.

HMS EXE

EXE was one of the first River class frigates, completed by Fleming and Ferguson (Paisley) in August 1942. The first 24 vessels of the class were fitted for minesweeping. She was fitted with five extra 20-mm guns for Operation Torch, the North African landings. She was placed in reserve in 1947 and in 1949 she was converted to be a Landing Ship Headquarters (Small). By 1954 all her armament, with the exception of her depth charge throwers, had been removed. She was broken up at Preston in September 1956.

HMS JED

JED was launched by Charles Hill of Bristol in July 1942. She was fitted with reciprocating engines. It had been planned to fit all the class with geared turbines, but there was insufficient capacity for the production of the turbine blades and so only half a dozen were so fitted. She served in the Atlantic and in operations off Burma. Placed in reserve in 1946, she was broken up at Milford Haven in July 1957.

HMS HELFORD

HELFORD completed in June 1943 by Hall Russell at Aberdeen. She did not carry minesweeping davits and was fitted with a funnel cowl. Note the searchlights on the bridge each side of the radar lantern. She served with the 3rd Escort Group out of Londonderry and then with the South Atlantic Escort Force prior to joining the Aden Escort Force. In November 1945 she left Aden for the UK and was placed in reserve at Devonport and later at Lisahally. The extra endurance in these ships over the earlier corvettes made them suitable for operations in the Indian Ocean. She was broken up at Troon in June 1956.

HMS NESS

The NESS was completed in December 1942 by Robb. She was fitted with minesweeping equipment aft, making her quarterdeck very cluttered. Earlier ships of the class were fitted with 8 depth charge throwers aft, but four were later removed. Whilst escorting convoy WS30/KMF 15 she took part in the sinking of the Italian submarine LEONARDO DA VINCI on 23 May1943 near Cape Finisterre. The Italian submarine had sunk 58,973 tons of shipping including the troop transport EMPRESS OF CANADA. NESS was broken up at Newport in 1956.

HMS WYE

WYE was completed in February 1944 by Robb. Some of this class were fitted with 8 depth charge throwers and carried over 200 depth charges. Compare that with the virtually empty quarterdecks of the following Loch class. The 4-inch gun in these ships had a range of 9,500 yards and was the same as that fitted in the Castle class corvettes. This shows the weatherly lines of these ships, which were built to cope with the North Atlantic gales. Post war she was in reserve at Harwich and later at Barrow-in-Furness. She was broken up at Faslane in 1955.

HMS ANGUILLA

The ANGUILLA, ex-HALLOWELL, ex-PF 72, was an American Tacoma class frigate, built on the lines of the British River class, but of all welded construction. They were slightly longer than the Rivers, and had a different bridge layout and mast arrangement, and carried a main armament of three open 3-inch guns. She was built by Walsh Kaiser and completed in October 1943. She helped sink U-286 on 29 April 1945 whilst part of Escort Group 19, carrying out a sweep of the approaches to Murmansk prior to the sailing of convoy RA 66. She was returned to the United States Navy in May 1946.

HMS ANTIGUA

ANTIGUA, ex-HAMMOND, ex-PF 73, was another of the American built Tacoma class frigates, called the Colony class in the Royal Navy. The American Navy did not pursue this class, preferring instead their own designs which had higher speeds. She was completed by Walsh Kaiser at Providence Rhode Island in November 1943. She was returned to the USN in May 1946.

HMS CALDER

Another American built frigate, this time to an American design. CALDER, of the Captain class, was completed in July 1943 at Bethlehem (Hingham). Her turbo electric propulsion developed 12,000 shaft horse-power giving her a speed of 26 knots. They were 306 ft long, and displaced 1,300 tons, comparable with the River class frigates in size. Their guns were three 3-inch in open mountings protected by bulwarks. Note the large amount of depth charge equipment aft. She shared the sinking of U-1172 in the Irish Sea in January 1945, and U-774 south west of Ireland in April 1945. She was returned to the USN in October 1945.

HMS MOUNSEY

MOUNSEY was a diesel electric driven version of the Captain class frigates built in the USA. Their engines developed 6,000 horse-power giving them a speed of 20 knots. They were slightly smaller than the turbo electric Captains, being 289.5 ft long, and displacing 1,085 tons. MOUNSEY was one of the class fitted with two rails for the Mk.X (heavy) depth charges. She completed at Boston in December 1943 and was returned to the USN in February 1946.

This scene shows the crew working at depth charges on the stern of an escort (in this case a sloop), showing the cluttered working area exposed to the elements. Possibly pleasant in the summer in a calm sea, but a nightmare when handling the heavy charges in the freezing winter gales of the North Atlantic.

The Hedgehog, the first operational ahead throwing anti-submarine weapon. This was mounted forward, it trebled the escorts killing chances, by firing the bombs whilst the escort still held contact with the enemy submarine. It was unpopular as it lacked the large explosions which boosted the morale of the crews of the escorts and nearby merchant ships. However, its benefits were eventually realised and it was to be fitted to all non-Squid fitted anti-submarine escorts by the end of the war.

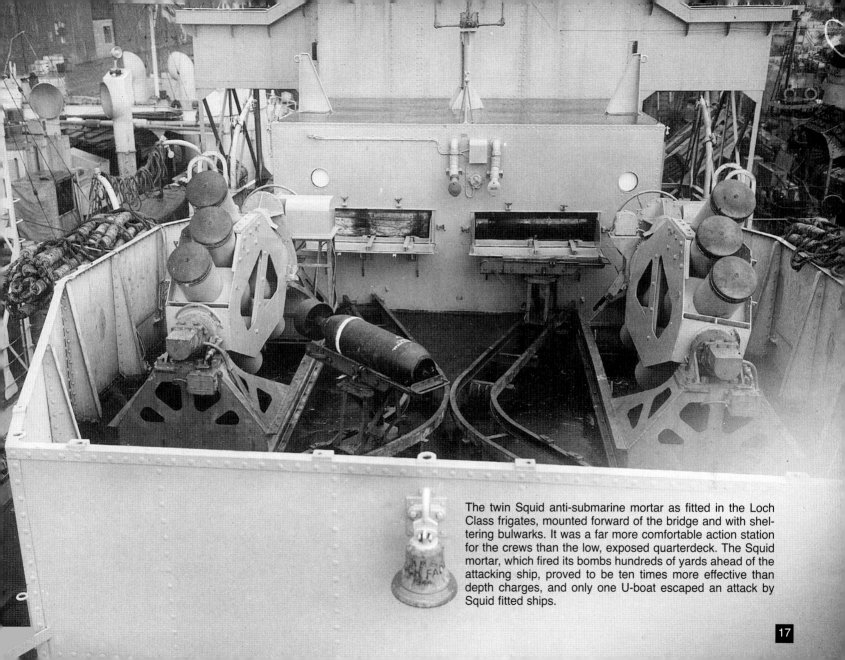

The twin Squid anti-submarine mortar as fitted in the Loch Class frigates, mounted forward of the bridge and with sheltering bulwarks. It was a far more comfortable action station for the crews than the low, exposed quarterdeck. The Squid mortar, which fired its bombs hundreds of yards ahead of the attacking ship, proved to be ten times more effective than depth charges, and only one U-boat escaped an attack by Squid fitted ships.

HMS LOCH CRAGGIE

LOCH CRAGGIE was launched in May 1944 by Harland and Wolff, and completed at Clydebank in October 1944, 8 months after being laid down, showing the value of the rapid production techniques employing prefabrication. She helped sink U-482 in the North Channel on 16 January 1945. She served in the East Indies later in the war, returning to the UK in October 1946. In 1950-52 she served in the Mediterranean. She was broken up at Lisbon in October 1963.

HMS LOCH DUNVEGAN

LOCH DUNVEGAN was completed by Hill of Bristol on 30 June 1944. She helped sink U-354, which had just damaged the carrier NABOB and sunk the frigate BICKERTON, on 24 August 1944 north of Murmansk., and U-989 on 14 February 1945 north of the Shetlands. Note the clear quarterdeck. These ships carried just two depth charge throwers and one rail. Post war she served with the Rosyth Flotilla. After a period in reserve she served in the Mediterranean 1950-52 before returning to the reserve fleet. She was broken up at Briton Ferry in August 1960.

HMS LOCH ECK

LOCH ECK completed on 7 November 1944 at Smith's Dock. She helped sink U-1279 on 3 February 1945 and U-989 on 14 February 1945, both north of the Shetlands. On 17 February 1945 she helped sink U-1278, again off the Shetlands. She was transferred to the Royal New Zealand Navy in October 1948. She was renamed HAWEA, and was in the Korean War from 1951-53. She was towed to Hong Kong for breaking up, arriving there in March 1966. Note the quadruple 2-pounder fitted aft rather than the second single 4-inch mounted in the earlier River class.

HMS LOCH FYNE
LOCH FYNE was completed in November 1944 at Burntisland. Note the radar mounted on a lattice foremast to clear the bridge and give a longer range. At the end of the war she was in the East Indies, returning to UK and being placed in reserve in June 1946. In 1950 she commissioned for the Home Fleet and took part in the search for the lost submarine AFFRAY in 1951 in the Channel. She was placed in reserve again in 1952. In 1953-54 she was modernised at Glasgow, as seen here. She was given a twin 4-inch gun forward and modern 40-mm AA guns, whilst her depth charge equipment was removed. She then served in the East Indies and Persian Gulf, paying off in May 1963. She was broken up at Newport in August 1970.

(MoD/Crown Copyright)

HMS LOCH GORM

LOCH GORM was built by Harland and Wolff, but completed on the Clyde in December 1944. These ships were armed with an old 4-inch gun with a range of 16,200 yards, a large improvement over the 4-inch fitted to the River class. At the end of the war she was in the East Indies. She paid off to reserve in 1946. She was selected for modernisation, but this was cancelled and she was sold for commercial use as the Greek ORION in October 1961. She was broken up in Yugoslavia in 1966. Note her weatherly lines, with a slightly more pronounced flare and increased sheer over the River class.

LOCH KILLIN

LOCH KILLIN completed in April 1944 at Burntisland and then joined the 10th Escort Group. After work up she joined the famous Second Escort Group and achieved the first Squid 'kill' on U-333 on 31 July 1944. She also helped sink U-608 at the entrance to the Channel and U-736 in the Bay of Biscay in August 1944, and U-1063 off Start Point in April 1945. She was placed in reserve in September 1945 at Dartmouth, and later at Penarth. She was selected for modernisation after the war, but this was cancelled and she was broken up at Newport in August 1960.

HMS LOCH LOMOND

LOCH LOMOND was completed in November 1944 by Caledon, 11 months after being laid down. At the end of the war she was in the East Indies, and in February 1946 scuttled U-862 in the Malacca Strait. She returned to the UK in March 1946 and served in the Mediterranean 1950-52. She was modernised at Bristol in 1953-54. She was photographed after this refit, with a twin 4-inch gun forward, and a twin 40-mm aft in place of the quadruple 2-pounder. She retained her two Squid mortars forward, but her depth charge gear aft was replaced by four saluting guns. She then served in the East Indies and Persian Gulf. On 1 September 1959 she became the last warship to commission at Sheerness before the closure of that yard. After a commission 1962-64 in the Far East she paid off in December 1964. She was towed to Faslane to be broken up in October 1968.   (MoD/Crown Copyright)

HMS LOCH VEYATIE

LOCH VEYATIE was completed by Ailsa in July 1946, the last Loch to be completed. She was fitted with a single Mk.24 4-inch gun forward. This had been designed for the Loch class frigates and Algerine class minesweepers, but was not available in time to be fitted to them all. This gun had a range of 19,400 yards. Her quarterdeck was cleared of depth charge equipment. In 1947 she was fitted with a modified bridge and a larger action information centre. From 1946-1955 she was used for anti-submarine training at Londonderry and Rosyth, and she carried the Red Hand of Ulster on her funnel indicating she was part of the Third Training Squadron. In 1956 she was placed in reserve at Lisahally. She was broken up at Dalmuir in August 1965.

HMS BURGHEAD BAY

Laid down as the LOCH HARPORT, BURGHEAD BAY was one of the Loch class altered to carry a mainly anti-aircraft armament, reflecting the shift of the focus of the war from the Atlantic to the Pacific. She was launched by Hill in March 1945, and was completed in September 1945, after the war was over. She carried a twin 4-inch gun forward and aft. The twin 4-inch mountings were taken from the laid up modernised V and W destroyers and also from Hunt class destroyers that were constructive total losses. She served in the Devonport Local Flotilla from 1944-52 and later in the South Atlantic and West Indies Station. She finally paid off in August 1958. She became the Portuguese ALVARES CABRAL in May 1959, and was sold in June 1971 for breaking up.

(MPL)

HMS MORECAMBE BAY
MORECAMBE BAY (ex LOCH HEILEN) was launched on 1 November 1946 by Pickersgill. She was completed by Samuel White in 1949. She served with distinction in the Korean War from 1950-53. In 1955 she joined the America and West Indies Station and later was placed in reserve at Lisahaly. She was sold to Portugal in 1961 and was renamed DON FRANCESCO DE ALMEIDA.

HMS ST. BRIDES BAY

ST. BRIDES BAY (ex-LOCH ACHILITY) was launched on 16 January 1945 and completed in June 1945 by Harland and Wolff, and was allocated to the British Pacific Fleet. In 1945 she joined the Mediterranean Fleet and was there until 1949, when she transferred to the 4th Frigate Squadron in the Far East. She took part in the Korean War from 1950-53, and recommissioned at Singapore in July 1960 using air trooping. She returned to the UK in December 1961 after 16 years in the Far East. She was broken up at Faslane in September 1962, the last of the Royal Navy's Bay class frigates. Note the twin 40-mm guns mounted each side amidships.   (MoD/Crown Copyright)

AFONSO DE ALBUQUEQUE (ex-DALRYMPLE)

One of the four Loch-Bay frigates completed as survey ships, DALRYMPLE, ex-LUCE BAY, ex-LOCH GLASS was launched by Pickersgill in December 1944 and completed at Devonport Dockyard in February 1949. She carried out surveys in the Persian Gulf and Far East in 1949-57, and was part of the salvage unit for Pt. Said in 1956. In 1959-63 she operated in the Persian Gulf, East Indies and Mediterranean and in 1963 in Home Waters. She paid off in November 1965. In April 1966 she transferred to Portugal and was renamed AFONSO DE ALBUQUERQUE. She was deleted in 1983 and was then used as an accommodation ship and was expended as target 1994, just after this photograph was taken at Alfeite Naval Base, Lisbon.

HMS SURPRISE

The SURPRISE was laid down as a Loch/Bay class frigate in April 1944, but was completed as a Despatch Vessel in September 1946, and joined the Mediterranean Fleet. She returned to the UK in 1953 where her twin 4-inch gun was temporarily replaced by a covered viewing platform whilst she was used as the Royal Yacht for the Coronation Review. Afterwards she returned to the Mediterranean remaining until December 1964. In 1959 she carried out trials with Whirlwind helicopters to test their capability in small ships. She arrived to be broken up at Bo'ness in June 1965. Her sister ship ALERT was allocated to the Far East Fleet. Note her ensign at half mast. (MoD/Crown Copyright)

HMS ARABIS

This modified Flower class corvette was completed by George Brown & Co., Greenock, in March 1944. She was transferred to the RNZN until April 1949, when she returned to the UK and was placed in reserve. She thus survived to be recategorised as a frigate. She was scrapped at Grays, Essex in August 1951. These later, slightly larger Flower class corvettes carried a single 4-inch gun and hedgehog and depth charges, but lacked the formidable Squid anti-submarine mortars that contemporary vessels carried. The Hedgehog mortar was mounted to starboard of the 4-inch gun. The handsome lines of these small vessels is clear is this view.

HMS CAISTOR CASTLE

The Castle class corvettes, later categorised as frigates, were of 1,010 tons and were 252 ft long, 47 ft more than the Flowers. This enabled them to carry the Squid anti-submarine mortar, mounted just abaft the single 4-inch gun. They carried their radar on a lattice mast. They were driven by one shaft, limiting their manoeuvrability, and their top speed was only 16.5 knots. CAISTOR CASTLE was completed in September 1944 by J.Lewis & Sons at Aberdeen. She was placed in reserve in 1947, and after a refit joined the Training Squadron at Portland 1953-55. She was at the Coronation Review in 1953. She paid off to reserve in 1955 and was broken up at Troon in March 1956. Because of their sea keeping qualities, several of these ships were taken into service as weather ships after the war.

HMS PELICAN

PELICAN was one of the pre-war sloops, completed in March 1939 by Thornycroft. Originally to have been built for survey duties, with the threatening war she was completed with four twin 4-inch guns and machine guns. Her early construction is indicated by the tripod foremast. She had geared turbines giving her a speed of 19.25 knots. During the war one of the after twin 4-inch guns was removed and a quadruple pom-pom fitted. She was mined in February 1941, and later helped escort convoys to the landings in North Africa. She sank U-438 in May 1943 in the Atlantic, and helped sink three others (U-136 in July 1942 off the Canary Islands, U-334 in June 1943 south west of Ireland and U-448 in April 1944 off Iceland). She survived the war to be recategorised as a frigate. She served in the Mediterranean to 1951, and then in the South Atlantic to 1957, when she paid off. She was sold for breaking up in November 1958.

HMS PEACOCK

PEACOCK was a modified Black Swan class sloop, completed by Thornycroft in May 1944. She was armed with three twin 4-inch guns and 12 –20mm, together with a heavy depth charge armament and hedgehog. She shared sinking U-354 in August 1944, U-394 in September 1944 and U-482 in January 1945. These vessels, despite their heavy AA armament, were good anti-submarine vessels, and had a speed of 20 knots (18.5 sea speed) and a range of 7,500 miles at 12 knots. Useful ships, she was allocated to the British Pacific Fleet but the war ended before she arrived. Post war she served in the Mediterranean and took part in Palestine patrols. She attended the Coronation Review in 1953 and paid off in 1954 and was broken up at Rosyth in May 1958.

HMS MERMAID

MERMAID was a modified Black Swan class sloop, completed in May 1944 by Denny at Dumbarton. She was fitted with twin 20-mm guns port and starboard amidships and on her quarterdeck, with single guns on sponsons abreast the bridge. She took part in convoys to Russia and helped sink U-354 in August 1944 and U-394 in September 1944, both in the Arctic, and was allocated to the British Pacific Fleet. She escorted a floating dock as far as Aden, but the war then ended so she returned to the Mediterranean, serving there until 1954, though returning home for the 1953 Coronation Review at Spithead. In May 1959 she was transferred to the German Navy and was renamed SCHARNHORST. She later was used as a damage control training hulk and was broken up at Zeebrugge in 1990.

HMS WHIMBREL

In the second group of the Black Swan class sloops, WHIMBREL was completed by Yarrow in January 1943, joining the famous Second Escort Group. With her good endurance and AA armament, she was fitted with hedgehog mortars, she served on Russian convoys and was in the Channel for the Normandy landings. In March 1945 she arrived at Colombo and in May 1945 joined the Fleet Train of the British Pacific Fleet Train, and took part in the Okinawa operations. She was transferred to the Egyptian Navy in 1949 and renamed EL MALEK FAROUQ. Renamed TARIK in 1954, she was only listed for sale in 2002, and attempts are being made to bring her back to the UK for preservation.

HMS OAKLEY

OAKLEY, ex TICKHAM, was a Type II Hunt class destroyer, completed by Yarrow in May 1942 after delays caused by bombing. She was armed with three twin 4-inch and four 2-pounders, 4 DCT. She was designed for 29 knots, with a sea speed of 25.5 knots at full load. She had a limited range of 3.150 miles at 15 knots. 86 of this class were built in all, in 4 types. She took part in Arctic convoy operations and was at the Sicilian landings. In December 1943 she grounded and repairs at Taranto took to April 1944. She then took part in the South of France landings and the re-occupation of Athens. She paid off in December 1945. She was transferred to West Germany 10.1958, renamed GNEISENAU, and used as a gunnery training ship. She was broken up in 1977.

HMS BRISSENDEN

BRISSENDEN was one of the two Type IV Hunt class destroyers. They were a large variation of the original Hunt design incorporating many new features, especially for the severe weather conditions of the Arctic. She was completed by Thornycroft on 12 February 1943. Of 1,175 tons, she carried 3 twin 4-inch, four 2-pounders and 8 –20mm guns as well as 3 torpedo tubes and 4 depth charge throwers and two rails, a formidable armament for so small a vessel. She was designed for 27 knots, and had a speed of 25 knots when at full load. She had a longer forecastle for improved strength and a knuckle in the bow. The covered deck amidships showed again in the River design, and later frigates. She served on Russian convoys and escorted convoys for the Normandy landings. She was in the Mediterranean 1945-46 and took part in the Palestine patrols. Placed in reserve in June 1948, she was scrapped in March 1965.

HMCS FORT ERIE

FORT ERIE was a Canadian built River class frigate, commissioning at Quebec City in October 1944, having been built by G.T.Davie. She operated out of Halifax, NS, with Escort Group 28. In 1946 she was sold, but later re-acquired. She was rebuilt in 1954-56 with an enclosed bridge, a twin 4-inch gun forward and twin Squid anti-submarine mortars aft. She also had an enlarged foremast, though still tripod in construction, and a taller funnel. Her hull was strengthened forward to cope with ice and her accommodation was improved. These modified Rivers were known as the Prestonian class. She served as a training ship until she paid off on 26 March 1965 at Halifax, and was broken up at La Spezia in 1966. The Royal Navy never modernised the River class, using instead the Fleet destroyers with their higher speeds more suitable for anti-submarine operations in the 1950s.

HMS ORWELL

ORWELL was completed as a Fleet destroyer in October 1942 by Thornycroft. She served on Russian Convoys 1942-45, taking part in the action against LUTZOW, HIPPER and 6 destroyers in December 1942. She also took part in the Normandy landings. She paid off in November 1947 and was converted to a Type 16 anti-submarine frigate at Rosyth in 1952, commissioning in December 1952. Her new armament comprised a twin 4-inch forward and twin squid aft, supplemented with seven 40-mm guns and four torpedo tubes. Her tubes were removed when she was employed as a minelayer. The minelaying stern is visible in this photograph. She retained her destroyer machinery, giving her a speed of 36.75 knots (31.25 sea speed). She served in the Plymouth local flotilla until being placed in reserve in 1958. She was towed to the breakers in June 1965.

(WSPL)

HMS PALADIN

The destroyer PALADIN was built at Chatham Dockyard and completed in December 1941. She took part in the Diego Suarez operations in May 1942, in Malta convoys and in actions against enemy surface units in the Mediterranean. She helped sink U-205 in February 1943 off Libya and the Japanese submarine I-27 in February 1944 in the Indian Ocean. In October 1945 she returned to the UK from the Far East and was placed in reserve. She was converted to a Type 16 frigate at Rosyth 1952-54. Her torpedo tubes were landed to enable her to operate as a minelayer. She was broken up on the Tyne in October 1962.

HMS TERPSICHORE

TERPSICHORE was built by Denny, and completed in January 1944. She helped sink U-407 in September 1944. In 1953-55 she was converted by Thornycroft to a Type 16 frigate, with an enclosed bridge in the style that was to be adopted by new construction frigates. Above the bridge was an open platform which could be used for gunnery control or as an open bridge. Two sister ships were also given this type of bridge, whilst four other sisters were converted retaining the standard destroyer bridge. She was scrapped at Troon in May 1966.

HMS URCHIN

URCHIN completed as a destroyer by Vickers-Armstrong Ltd at Barrow in September 1943. She served in the Mediterranean and at Normandy, and in December 1944 joined the British Pacific Fleet and took part in operations at Okinawa and against the Japanese mainland in 1945. She underwent a full conversion to Type 15 at Barclay Curle, Glasgow in 1952- May 1954, being fitted with Limbo anti-submarine mortars. She was placed in reserve in 1956 and in 1959 was refitted with an upper, open bridge for her role in the Dartmouth Training Squadron. He paid off in August 1964. In 1966, by when she had been laid up, her stern was removed and fitted to her sister ship ULSTER. She was broken up at Troon in August 1967.

HMS WIZARD

WIZARD completed as a fleet destroyer in March 1944 at Barrow. She took part in operations off the Norwegian coast and off Normandy. In June 1944 she was accidently damaged by her own depth charges, and repairs at Middlesbrough took to May 1945. She reached the Far East in time to be present for the surrender of Japan. Post war she served in home waters. In 1953-July 1954 she underwent conversion to a Type 15 at Devonport Dockyard, being fitted with Limbo mortars. She joined the 3rd Training Squadron and in 1956 paid off to be refitted with an extra, open bridge like URCHIN, for her role in the Dartmouth Training Squadron in the 1960s. This also entailed the removal of the forward (twin 40mm) gun. She paid off in December 1965, and was sold for breaking up in February 1967.

HMS URSA

URSA completed as a fleet destroyer at Thornycroft's in March 1944. She undertook operations off the Norwegian coast and was at Normandy. Afterwards she was in several actions with surface ships off the French coast, when enemy ships were sunk or damaged. In October 1944 she sailed for the Far East and took part in the raid on Palembang in February 9145 and the actions at Okinawa in May 1945. In 1946 she returned to the UK to pay off. She underwent full conversion to frigate at Palmers, Tyne from 1953 to August 1955, being equipped with a twin 4-inch gun, a twin 40-mm gun and two Limbo anti-submarine mortars. These ships were also fitted with a large operations room abaft the bridge. She served in the Mediterranean and West Indies, providing aid at the Lebanon earthquake disaster in 1956. She was damaged in a collision with the destroyer BATTLEAXE in August 1962. She arrived to be broken up at Newport on 25 September 1967.

HMS UNDAUNTED

The UNDAUNTED completed at Cammell Lairds in March 1944. She took part in operations off Norway, at Normandy and in December 1944 joined the British Pacific Fleet for operations against Japan. She was fully converted to an anti-submarine frigate by White 1952-June 1954. She was attached to the Underwater Defence Establishment at Portland. For a period in 1958 she carried three fixed anti-submarine torpedo tubes on her starboard side. She was also fitted with a helicopter deck for trials with the P531 helicopter (prototype of the Wasp). She paid off in July 1974 and was used for Exocet trials and was finally sunk by Exocet and torpedoes from NORFOLK and SWIFTSURE off Gibraltar in November 1978.

HMS TROUBRIDGE

TROUBRIDGE was completed in March 1943 by Clydebank as a fleet destroyer. In September 1944 she helped sink U-407 and once spent 93 days continuously at sea, a record for a destroyer. She underwent full conversion, starting at Portsmouth Dockyard in August 1953 and being completed by J. Samuel White in July 1957. She was one of several type 15s fitted with the twin 40-mm forward and a new style enclosed bridge just abaft it. She was equipped with Limbo anti-submarine mortars. She was sold for breaking up and arrived at Newport in May 1970.

47

HMS BLACKWOOD

A Type 14 second rate A/S frigate, designed for fast construction. Completed in August 1957 by Thornycroft – F78 – she was armed with two Limbo anti-submarine mortars and three 40-mm guns. Note the enclosed bridge and bulwark sheltering hands when working on the forecastle. She first commissioned as target for the Third Submarine Squadron and then became a training ship at Portland. In 1965-67 she was employed on fishery protection, when her hull was damaged by ice. In 1967 she became a harbour training ship at Portsmouth, and in 1968 an accommodation ship at Rosyth before returning to her training role at Portsmouth. She was arrived at Troon to be broken up in November 1976. She was named after one of the best known frigate Captains of Nelson's era.

HMS DUNCAN

DUNCAN was completed in October 1958 by Thornycroft, the last of the class of 12 to complete. DUNCAN was powered by a single propeller, giving a speed of 27.8 knots. This single shaft arrangement was reminiscent of the early corvettes, and made manoeuvring more difficult. From 1958-65 she was leader of the Fishery protection Squadron. She later was an anti-submarine training ship at Londonderry and then Portland. In 1971 she became a harbour training ship at Portsmouth. She was broken up on the Medway in 1985.

HMS DUNDAS

DUNDAS was completed in March 1956 by Samuel White. The hulls of these vessels were found to be too weak for the severe weather they encountered on fishery protection duties off Iceland, and they had to be strengthened. Their single screw limited their manoeuvrability. Note the clear forecastle with the single 40-mm guns each side of the foremast. She served in the Second Frigate Squadron at Portland and later took part in Fishery Protection off Iceland. In 1978 she was placed in reserve at Chatham and became an accommodation ship at Portsmouth in 1979. She was towed from Portsmouth on 24 April 1983 for breaking up at Troon.   (MoD/Crown Copyright)

HMS HARDY

The first of the class, she was completed in December 1955 by Yarrow. The distinctive bow was designed to make them more able to cope with anti-submarine operations in heavy weather, as was their enclosed bridge. Later the third gun (on the quarterdeck) was removed. She served in the Third Training Squadron at Londonderry 1955-58 and then in the Second Frigate Squadron at Portland, with spells in the Stand By Squadron. In 1979 she became a stores and accommodation ship at Portsmouth for ships under refit. She was sunk as a target in the Atlantic in July 1983, being fired on with Exocet, gunfire and torpedoes. (MoD/Crown Copyright)

HMS EXMOUTH

EXMOUTH was completed by Samuel White in December 1957. She spent her first year in operational reserve and then was a submarine target on the Clyde from 1958. In 1963 she joined the Fishery Protection Squadron. In April 1966 she was taken in hand at Chatham for a two year refit to install gas turbine engines. She was given an Olympus engine developing 15,000 shp, and two Proteus developing 3,650 shp each. She could then be distinguished by the extra air intakes and streamlined funnel. She was fitted with controllable pitch propellers and had a speed of 28 knots. She undertook cold weather trials in 1969 and in December 1976 was placed in reserve. She was scrapped at Briton Ferry in February 1979. (MoD/Crown Copyright)

HMS BLACKPOOL

The Type 12 frigate BLACKPOOL was completed by Harland and Wolff on 12 August .1958. Note the anti-submarine torpedo tubes fitted on the upper deck abreast the after gun. She transferred to the Royal New Zealand Navy in 1966 when that Navy paid off the cruiser ROYALIST. She was present at the Fiji Independence Celebrations in October 1970. She returned to the Royal Navy in 1971 and paid off. Her 4..5-inch turret was removed in 1971. She was used for sonar dome shock trials in 1974, and in 1976 left Portsmouth under tow for further trials. An extra mast was .fitted forward in 1977 for target trials. She was broken up in the Forth in May 1978 after use for underwater explosive trials.

(MoD/Crown Copyright)

HMS EASTBOURNE

EASTBOURNE was launched by Vickers-Armstrong Ltd., Tyne and completed in January 1958 at Barrow. She was the only one of the Whitby class fitted with stabilisers. She undertook Fishery protection duties and served in the Far East. She is carrying 6 anti-submarine torpedo tubes on each side of her upper deck in this photograph. In 1964 she joined the Dartmouth Training Squadron, being fitted with extra deckhouses and boats. In the 1972-73 her turret, mortars and gunnery director were removed. In 1976 she took part in the Cod War off Iceland and was holed in a collision with the gunboat BALDUR. In 1979-80 she was fitted with paddle wheels for alongside training at Rosyth. She was broken up by White in March 1985.

HMS TORQUAY

TORQUAY was the first Type 12 to complete, in May 1956 by Harland and Wolff. She took part in the 1956 Suez operations. She joined the Dartmouth Training Squadron in 1962, with extra deckhouses aft. Later she was given an enclosed foremast and the after deckhouse was extended and a Limbo mortar removed. In 1972-83 she was a navigation and direction training and trials ships. She became a Harbour Training ship at Devonport prior to being towed to be broken up at Barcelona on 1 July 1987. She was therefore both the first and last of the Whitby class. Her sister, SCARBOROUGH, seen beyond, retained her original upright funnel.

HMS TENBY

TENBY completed in December 1957 at Cammell Laird. These ships had two Limbo mortars in a well amidships, which led on to an exposed, low quarterdeck. Their after gun was originally a twin, radar controlled 40-mm, but they were later replaced by single 40-mm. She achieved 30.96 knots on trials, the fastest of her class. She served in home waters and the Mediterranean. In November 1962 she joined the Dartmouth Training Squadron, with extra boats and a deckhouse aft. She paid off in December 1970. A sale to Pakistan was not concluded, and she was broken up at Briton Ferry in September 1977.

HMS WHITBY

WHITBY was completed in July 1956 by Cammell Laird. She is seen here with her original, upright funnel. She had a slightly different style of bridge to her sisters. She served in the Third Training Squadron at Londonderry and then on General Service Commissions in home waters, Mediterranean and Far East, and also in the South Atlantic. The voyage to Capetown was a challenge to her endurance of 3,300 miles at 12 knots. She undertook Cod War patrols in 1973 and was damaged in a collision with the gunboat THOR in September 1973. She paid off in December 1974. She was broken up at Queenborough in January 1979.

HMCS MACKENZIE

The Canadian Navy had designed and built their own destroyer escorts (frigates) post war. Their vessels were flush decked, with a twin 3-inch gun forward and aft, enclosed bridge, anti-submarine torpedo tubes and Limbo mortars aft. They also incorporated a raised forecastle, though not so pronounced as that in the Whitby class (where clearance was required for the 4.5-inch gun). They had a speed of 28 knots. Their upperdecks and upperworks had rounded edges to allow the fast dispersal of water and reduce the formation of ice. MACKENZIE was typical, built by Canadian Vickers Ltd, Montreal, she commissioned on 6 October 1962. She underwent a major refit in 1986-87 and finally paid off in August 1993. She was scuttled off Sidney, Vancouver Island, in May 1995 to create an artificial reef after being used in the filming of the 'X-Files'.

HMS LYNX

The first of the Type 41 Anti-Aircraft frigates to complete, in March 1957, LYNX was built by J Brown on Clydeside. She was armed with two twin 4.5-inch guns and two 40-mm. A Seacat missile system was fitted later. These ships also carried a squid anti-submarine mortar, fitted on the quarterdeck. The class had rounded deck edges to allow water to run clear when pre-wetting to reduce radio activity from fall-out accumulating on the upper decks. She was the last RN ship to be based at Simonstown. In 1974-81 she was part of the Stand By Squadron at Chatham. She was sold to Bangladesh in March 1982 and renamed ABU BAKR, and was still extant in 2003.

HMS LEOPARD

These AA frigates had the same large forecastle for improved seakeeping as the Type 12s, leading to a sharp drop in level to where the forward twin 4.5-inch turret was sited. The low bridge just allowed visibilty across the high cable deck. LEOPARD completed in December 1958, having been built at Portsmouth. Later her mainmast was plated in and she was given new radar, with a single 40-mm gun sited abaft the mainmast. In July 1963 she was damaged in a collision with the South African minesweeper PIETERMARITZBURG off Cape Point. She was repaired at Portsmouth 1963-64. In 1975 she took part in the Third Cod War off Iceland. She paid off in January 1976 and was broken up at Dartford in October 1977.   (MoD/Crown Copyright)

HMS JAGUAR

JAGUAR was completed in December1959 by Denny, the last warship to be built by that firm. She was the last of four Type 41 AA frigates to be completed for the Royal Navy. A fifth ship, the PANTHER, was completed for India as the BRAMA-PUTRA. These ships had diesel engines, their funnel exhaust being integrated with their mast structures. The diesels gave them a maximum speed of 25 knots and an endurance of 7,850 miles at 15 knots. The higher speed of the Type 12s, which had steam propulsion, was not considered necessary for the role of these vessels. They were still very large by early frigate standards, almost 340ft long and with a displacement of 2,300 tons. She took part in the 1973 Cod War with bows strengthened by railway sleepers, as seen in this photograph. In October 1973 she joined the Stand By Squadron. She recommissioned in 1976 for operations off Iceland in the next Cod War. JAGUAR was transferred to Bangladesh in July 1978 and renamed ALI HAIDER. She was extant in 2003.

(MoD/Crown Copyright)

HMS LLANDAFF

Seven of these Aircraft Direction frigates (Type 61) were planned, but only 4 completed. LLANDAFF was built by Hawthorn Leslie & Co., Newcastle and completed in April 1958. Similar to the type 41 AA frigates in size and construction, they were again diesel engined with exhausts integrated in the masts. Her after STAAG mounting was replaced by a twin 40-mm(Mk 5) later. In 1966 her foremast and mainmast were covered over. LLANDAFF was sold to Bangladesh in December 1976 and renamed UMAR FEROOQ. She was due to be stricken in 1998, but was refitted and still extant in 2003.

HMS SALISBURY

SALISBURY was an Aircraft Direction frigate built at Devonport Dockyard and completed in February 1957. This photograph, taken in 1962, shows her slightly modernised with 965 radar and main mast plated in, with a STAAG 40-mm gun mounting aft of the radar offices and arrays. Note the Squid mounting aft on the quarterdeck. In 1967 she stood by during disturbances in the West Indies. She was damaged in a collision with the destroyer DIAMOND in the Channel in 1976.

HMS SALISBURY

From 1967-70 SALISBURY was modernised, with more powerful radar which increased her top hamper. A Seacat missile system replaced the STAAG mounting aft, and both her masts (Smacks) were plated in. In 1976 she was damaged in collisions with the Icelandic Gunboats TYR and AEGIR in the Third Cod War. She was offered for sale to Egypt in 1978, but negotiations fell through at the last minute. She became a training ship at Devonport 1980-85. In September 1985 she was sunk as target west of Ireland, being sunk by bombs, missiles and torpedo.

F117

HMS ASHANTI

The Tribal class frigates were general purpose vessels. ASHANTI was the first, completing in November 1961 by Yarrow. They were unusual for RN ships in being flush decked. They were armed with two single 4.5-inch guns taken from old destroyers, and carried a helicopter. Her single Limbo mortar can be seen forward of her flight deck. She had single 40-mm guns each side of the bridge. An unusual feature for that time was the provision of dining halls for the crew. These ships introduced full air conditioning and all bunk sleeping arrangements. In March 1977 she was extensively damaged by a fire in her boiler room in the Bristol Channel. She paid off in May 1977 and in 1981 became a harbour training ship at Portsmouth. ASHANTI was sunk as a target in September 1988.

HMS MOHAWK

MOHAWK was launched by Vickers-Armstrongs at Barrow in April 1962, and completed on the Tyne in November 1963. As with the other Tribal class frigates, she had a single Limbo anti-submarine mortar to supplement the helicopter for anti-submarine duties. 360ft in length, they were slightly smaller than the Type 12 frigates, and displaced 2,300 tons. In this view the covers for the hanger which was below the flight deck can be seen. The whole arrangement for the helicopter and Limbo mortar was very tight. In 1970 it was planned to remove her after gun and helicopter to make room for duties in the Dartmouth Training Squadron, but this refit was cancelled. In 1979 she joined the Stand By Squadron. MOHAWK was sold for breaking up in September 1982.

HMS ZULU

ZULU was completed by Stephen in April 1964, and hence was the last Type 81 completed. These ships had both a steam boiler and turbines and gas turbines, driving a single propeller. This gave them the ability to get under weigh at short notice, and a maximum speed of 25.25 knots, with a range of 5,300 miles at 12 knots. Again, like the Type 14 and the corvettes, their single screw reduced their manoeuvrability. ZULU was fitted with two Seacat AA missile systems and two Oelikons, as can be seen in this photograph. Brought forward from reserve in 1982 to release other ships for the Falklands War, she was sold in April 1984 to Indonesia and renamed MARTHA KHRYSTINA TIYAHADU. She was deleted in 2000.

F124

HMS MERMAID

This unique frigate was ordered from Yarrow by the Ghanaian government as the BLACK STAR. The order was cancelled in 1966 and she was launched in December 1966 to clear the slipway. She was taken over by the Royal Navy in 1972, and after a refit at Chatham was commissioned in the Royal navy in 1973 as MERMAID. Of flush deck design, with a twin 4-inch forward and two single 40-mm guns and a Limbo mortar aft, she was diesel driven and had a speed of 24 knots. Her hull was virtually the same size as the Type 41/61 frigates. She took part in the Cod Wars off Iceland, being in collision with the gunboats THOR and TYR in 1976. The minesweeper FITTLETON sank after a collision with her in 1976. She was sold to the Royal Malaysian Navy in May 1977 and renamed HANG TUAH, and is still extant (2003). (PRNM)

HMS RHYL

A repeat of the Type 12, Whitby class, frigates, the Rothesay class comprised 9 ships. RHYL was one of this class, being built at Portsmouth Dockyard, completing in October 1960. Their design was virtually the same as the original Type 12s, except they had a modified after super-structure with a single 40-mm gun mounted high up aft. Originally their anti-submarine capability depended on Limbo mortars and anti-sub-marine torpedoes. RHYL took part in the Mozambique Channel patrol in 1966 and the Cyprus evacuation in 1974. RHYL was modernised at Devonport, completing in May 1972 with a helicopter deck. She was expended as a target in August 1985.   (MoD/Crown Copyright)

HMS LOWESTOFT

LOWESTOFT was completed in October 1961 by Stephen. She took part in the Mozambique Channel patrol in 1966. She was modernised at Chatham, completing in June 1970. The after mast was plated in and she had a hanger and flight deck. She then carried a Wasp helicopter, and had only one Limbo mounting. She also had a new gunnery system with a new gunnery director. In 1975 she helped evacuate refugees from Vietnam. In 1975 and 1976 she undertook Cod War patrols and was damaged in collision with the gunboat THOR in 1976. She attended the International Naval review for the US Bicentennial off New York in July 1976. In 1976-77 she was refitted at Portsmouth as a towed array trials ship. She was expended as a target for Tigerfish torpedo in June 1986.

(MoD/Crown Copyright)

HMS ROTHESAY

This is an aerial view of the ROTHESAY, which was completed by Yarrow in April 1960. She was the first of the class to be modernised. The work was carried out at Rosyth between May 1966 and May 1968. The single Limbo arrangement is clearly visible here. In March 1969 she landed troops at Anguilla. In 1973 she took part in Cod War patrols, and in 1981 undertook Gulf patrols. In 1985 she became part of the Dartmouth Training Squadron and after 800, 000 miles steaming paid off in March 1988. She left Portsmouth on 1 November 1988 in tow for Spain to be broken up at Santander.

HMS LONDONDERRY

LONDONDERRY was built by Samuel White, completing in July 1960. She was modernised at Rosyth, completing in February 1970. In 1975-79 she was refitted for use as a trials ship for ASWE and in October 1979 re-commissioned as a radar trials ship. In 1984 she was used for Dartmouth Training. She was used for trials of pump jet propulsion and in became a harbour training ship at Portsmouth in 1984 to 1988. In this view she is disarmed and has extra masts fitted for trials. She was sunk as target for bombing, missiles and gunfire in June 1989.   (MoD/Crown Copyright)

HMS PENELOPE

PENELOPE was photographed on trials on the Tyne on 11 July 1963 with the short funnel originally designed for this class. She was completed in October 1963 by Vickers-Armstrong. In 1967 she became a trials ship for the Admiralty Underwater Weapons Establishment and her armament was put in preservation. She was used for noise trials and also was towed by SCYLLA at 23 knots in 1970. In 1973 she was selected for Seawolf missile trials, with her 4.5-inch gun removed and extra deckhouses fitted aft. In 1978 to 1982 she was modified with Exocet at Devonport, and in 1982 took part in the Falklands War. She was in collision with the Canadian ship PRESERVER off Norway in 1988, receiving a 40 x 4 ft gash in her side. She was sold to Ecuador in April 1991, being renamed PRESIDENTE ELOY ALFARO.   (MPL)

HMS NAIAD

The LEANDER Class were a follow on from the ROTHESAY class in hull form, though with no low quarterdeck. Instead, they were built to carry helicopters in a hangar incorporated into their superstructure. NAIAD was in the first group, completing by Yarrow March 1965. She was the first Leander equipped with Seacat missiles. From January 1973-June 1975 at Devonport she was fitted with Ikara anti-submarine missile forward in place of her twin 4.5-inch gun. In 1976 she was damaged in collision with the gunboat TYR off Iceland and in 1977 she was at the Silver Jubilee Review of the Fleet. She paid off in May 1987 and then was used for damage control and blast trials, being renamed HUL VUL, and was expended as a target in September 1990.

(MoD/Crown Copyright)

HMS DANAE

DANAE was in the second group of 6 Leander class frigates, being fitted with improved machinery. She completed in September 1967 at Devonport Dockyard. She was built with a well aft for variable depth sonar, but this was never fitted and the well was plated in later. From August 1977 to April 1981 she was refitted at Devonport with Exocet missiles in place of her 4.5-inch gun. She also carried two triple anti-submarine torpedo tubes to replace the Limbo mortar, which had been removed in order to enlarge the hangar and flight deck to accommodate the Lynx helicopter which was replacing the smaller Wasp. In this view her helicopter can be seen on her flight deck. She mounted Seacat on her hangar. She was sold to Ecuador in April 1991 and renamed MORAN VALVERDE.

HMS JUPITER

JUPITER was in the third group of Leander class, comprising 10 ships, all with improved boiler systems. She was completed in June 1969 by Yarrow. She stood by during unrest in Trinidad in 1970, and again at St. Lucia in 1972. In 1973 she undertook Cod War patrols. She was fitted with Seawolf and Exocet missiles in Devonport from January 1980 to October 1983. She was also fitted with two triple anti-submarine torpedo tubes. Note the sonar well at her stern. In 1986 she was one of the ships which evacuated refugees from South Yemen. In August 1990 she was sailed from Mombasa to patrol in the Gulf when the threat of a war there loomed. She paid off in April 1992 and was broken up at Alang in May 1998.

HMS EURYALUS

EURYALUS was in the first group of the Leander class, completing in September 1964 by Scots. She was converted to carry the Ikara missile system at Devonport from May 1973 to March 1976. She carried two Seacat missile systems on her hangar roof. 40-mm guns were mounted each side of the bridge. In October 1972 she towed a Greek tanker to safety after it had run aground in the Mozambique Channel. She served with the Dartmouth Training Squadron 1987-89. When she paid off she had steamed 700,000 miles plus, the lost of any Leander. She was broke up in Cumbria starting in September 1990. (MoD/Crown Copyright)

HMS LEANDER

LEANDER was originally to have been the Type 12- ROTHESAY class frigate WEYMOUTH. She was completed in March 1963 by Harland and Wolff. She was converted to carry Ikara from June 1970 to January 1973 at Devonport. In this photograph she can be seen firing an Ikara missile. In 1976 her bow was damaged in a collision with the gunboat THOR during a Cod War and lost all power whilst returning to UK in a 60-knot gale. She paid off in 1986 into the Stand By Squadron at Portsmouth and was expended as a target for Sea Dart and Exocet missiles and bombs in September 1989 during Exercise 'Sharp Spear'.

HMS ARGONAUT

ARGONAUT was in the second group of the Leander class, completing by Hawthorn Leslie in September 1967. She escorted RMS QUEEN MARY on the liner's final voyage to the USA. In 1974 she helped evacuate British citizens from Cyprus after the Turkish invasion. In December 1975 she was in collision with the gunboat TYR off Iceland. She was refitted to carry Exocet missiles from February 1976 to March 1980 at Devonport. In 1982 she was badly damaged by air attacks in the Falklands War. She was repaired at Devonport, and this was extended to a refit until 1983 during which she was fitted with a Type 2031 towed array sonar system. Note she carried Seacat missiles forward and aft. She paid off in March 1993, the last Leander in service, and was broken up in Spain in January 1995.

HMS CLEOPATRA

CLEOPATRA was built at Devonport Dockyard and completed in March 1966. Of the first group of the Leanders, she was modernised to carry Exocet missiles at Devonport from July 1973 to December 1975, the first Leander to be fitted with these missiles. From December 1981 to September 1983 she was refitted again at Devonport to carry Seacat and a Type 2031 towed array. The extra equipment then precluded her carrying a helicopter. She carried anti-submarine torpedo tubes in lieu of her Limbo mortar. Note the single 40-mm mounted each side of the bridge. She paid off in January 1992 and was towed to Alang in India to be broken up, arriving in January 1994.

HMS SIRIUS

SIRIUS was in the second group of Leander class, completed in June 1966. She was the last warship built in Portsmouth Dockyard. In 1970 she won the Wilkinson Sword of Peace for her work in rescue operations after a ferry disaster in the Caribbean. She was converted to carry Exocet missiles from March 1975 to February 1978 at Devonport. Her anti-submarine torpedo tubes were mounted a deck lower than in previous Leander conversions. From 1981 to 1983 she again refitted at Devonport to carry a Type 2031 towed array sonar system. In 1988 she attended the Australian centennial celebrations. She paid off February 1993 and was expended as a target in September 1998.

HMS HERMIONE

HERMIONE was launched by Stephen in April 1967 and completed at Yarrow. She was in the third group of the class, which were two feet wider in the beam than the earlier groups. She started a modernisation at Chatham in January 1980 to June 1983 to carry Seawolf and Exocet missiles in place of the original guns. Her masts and funnels were cut down to save weight. The refit was completed at Devonport in January 1984. In 1985 she was fitted with a deckhouse aft for electronic warfare equipment trials. She, like many of her sisters, served on patrols in the Persian Gulf. She paid off in June 1992 and arrived at Alang in May 1998 to be broken up.

HMS ANDROMEDA

ANDROMEDA was the first of third group of the Leander class. She was completed at Portsmouth in January 1969. She was fitted with a variable depth sonar, but this was later removed and the well aft plated in. In 1970 she was the first ship on the scene when the RFA ENNERDALE sank off the Seychelles. In 1973 she was damaged in collision with the gunboat ODINN and in 1974 helped evacuate British citizens from Cyprus. In 1976 she was damaged in a collision with a gunboat THOR during a later Cod War. She was modernised with Seawolf and Exocet missiles at Devonport from March 1978 to February 1981. She then had new funnels and masts and an enlarged hangar. She took part in the Falklands War and later served on patrols in the Gulf. She transferred to the Indian Navy in August 1995 and was renamed KRISHNA. (MoD/Crown Copyright)

HMS ARIADNE

ARIADNE was the last of the Leander class, being launched by Yarrow on 10 September 1971. She was never modified, and retained her twin 4.5 inch gun throughout her career, She was the last RN ship so fitted and carried out the last firing off the Isle of Wight on 10 April 1992. She was also the last RN ship to fire the Limbo anti-submarine mortar. She was part of the Standing Naval Force Atlantic in 1979 and also served in the West Indies. She was sold to Chile and sailed on 15 June 1992 as GENERAL BAQUEDANO. She paid off in 1998.

(MoD/Crown Copyright)

HMShips AMAZON and ANTELOPE (see Page 86)

AMAZON (foreground) was completed in May 1974 by Vosper Thornycroft. These frigates were known as the Type 21s. They carried a single 4.5inch gun of a new design and a helicopter. They were designed to carry Exocet missiles forward of their bridge, and most ships were fitted with these later. They were propelled by all gas turbine engines. Their hulls had to be strengthened in the 1980s. AMAZON was damaged by a fire in her engine room in November 1977. Repairs were carried out at Singapore. In 1980 she hit an uncharted pinnacle off Belize. She paid off in July 1993 and was sold to Pakistan in September 1993 and renamed BABUR.

HMS ANTELOPE
ANTELOPE was completed in June 1975. These were fast ships driven by Olympus and Tyne gas turbines giving a speed of 34 knots and good acceleration. In 1981 she seized £30 million of marijuana from a cargo vessel. She was hit by bombs in San Carlos water on 23 May 1982 during the Falklands War. The bomb exploded later that day and she caught fire and broke her back, sinking the next day.

HMS ARROW

ARROW was completed in May 1976 by Yarrow. Soon after completion, these ships had to have extra ballast added to counter topweight. In the 1980s their hulls were strengthened and tramsom flaps were added to reduce hull resistance, improving their speed by about a knot, and reducing fuel consumption. She took part in the Falkland War in 1982, bombarding during the operation to capture Goose Green and helping to fight fires on the stricken SHEFFIELD. Her hull was strengthened in 1983. She was sold to Pakistan in March 1994 and renamed KHAIBUR.

(MoD/Crown Copyright)

HMS ARDENT

ARDENT was completed in September 1977 by Yarrow. That year she received a 12 ft. gash in her bow during a collision with the Panamanian merchant ship FRISO off Portsmouth. During the Falklands War in 1982 she was hit and set on fire on 21 May while bombarding Goose Green. Fires started aft and grew out of control and she had to be abandoned. She sank overnight.   (MoD/Crown Copyright)

F184

HMS BROADSWORD

The BROADSWORD was the first Type 22 frigate. They were all gas turbine powered and all missile frigates. They were the first warships for Royal Navy to be specified and built in metric units, and the first with all missile armament, though 40-mm added later. At 3,556 tons and length 430 ft, they were enormously large in comparison with the Rivers. BROADSWORD was completed in February 1979 by Yarrow. In 1980 she aided yachts caught in bad weather during the Fastnet race. She took part in the Falklands War 1982, being damaged in air attacks, and rescuing 170 of the crew of the destroyer COVENTRY. In 1995 she recovered smuggled drums of cocaine from the sea in the West Indies. She paid off in March 1995, was sold to Brazil and renamed GREENHALGH. (MoD/Crown Copyright)

F88

HMS BRILLIANT
BRILLIANT was completed in May 1981 by Yarrow. She had a different funnel to BROADSWORD. Her gas turbines (Olympus and Tyne) could drive her at 30 knots. Note the bulwarks forward to protect men working on the forecastle. She served in the Falklands War 1982 and in the Kuwait Operations in 1991. This photograph was taken in the Gulf in 1991 with extra mine lookouts on watch. She was sold to Brazil and renamed DODSWORH in 1996.

(Steve Bush)

HMS LONDON

LONDON was the fourth of six Batch II Type 22 frigates. She was laid down in April 1982 as BLOODHOUND, but was renamed before her launch by Yarrow on 27 October 1984. This batch was 17.2 metres longer than the Batch I ships. LONDON's larger hangar and flight deck are clearly visible in this view. She took part in the Gulf operations in 1990 and the Kuwait operation in 1991. She underwent a major refit in Devonport in 1994-95 after covering 266,000 nautical miles. She paid off in June 1999 and was laid up at Portsmouth. She was sold to Romania in January 2003, and scheduled to be transferred in May 2005 after a refit at Portsmouth by Fleet Support Limited.   (MoD/Crown Copyright)

HMS CUMBERLAND

CUMBERLAND was in the third group of the Type 22 frigates, being accepted at Portsmouth on 19 November 1988. This group carried a single 4.5-inch gun forward and were also armed with Harpoon and Seawolf missiles, carried anti-submarine torpedo tubes and two Lynx or one Sea King helicopter. She had been ordered in 1982 to replaces losses in the Falklands War. In April 1989 she was the first ship to go alongside the new Weston Mill Lake Jetty at Devonport. In 2001 she was armed with the new electrically powered 4.5-inh gun mounting.

(MoD/Crown Copyright)

HMS NORFOLK

The NORFOLK was the first type 23 frigate, being completed in November 1989 by Yarrow and being commissioned in June 1990. Displacing 3,100 tons and 436ft. long, these frigates have gas turbine engines giving them a speed of 28 knots. They are built for silent running and anti-submarine operations, and have diesel electric propulsion giving them a speed of 15 knots. Their hulls include a 7 degrees slope to all vertical surfaces and rounded edges, reduction of infra red radiations and a hull bubble system to reduce radiated noise. She had a modified 4.5-inch gun fitted in 2001.   (MoD/Crown Copyright)

93

HMS ARGYLL

ARGYLL was built by Yarrow Shipbuilders on the Clyde, being ,launched on 8 April 1989 and commissioning on 31 May 1991. These handsome ships are armed with a single 4.5 inch gun forward, together with 8 McDonnell Douglas Harpoon missiles and British Aerospace vertical launch Seawolf GWS 26 Mod 1 missiles with 32 cannisters. They also carry a helicopter and anti-submarine torpedo tubes and are very effective all-round ships.

HMS ST. ALBANS
ST. ALBANS was laid down on 18 April 1999, launched on 6 May 2000 and completed on 6 June 2002, by Yarrow Shipbuilders, Glasgow. She is the last of the Type 23 frigates, and at present there is no follow on class of frigates, and so she is the last frigate. She has two twin anti-submarine torpedo tubes, and two 30-mm guns each side of her funnel. She can carry a Lynx of Merlin helicopter. She has a range of 7,800 miles at 15 knots and a crew of 181.

(Maritime Photographic)

INDEX